SEEK & FIND

BIOMES

TUNDRA · ALPINE · FOREST · RAINFOREST · SAVANNA
GRASSLAND · DESERT · FRESHWATER · MARINE

JORRIEN PETERSON

GIBBS SMITH
TO ENRICH AND INSPIRE HUMANKIND

For Tiera,
because I love
the adventures
we have together.

FIRST EDITION
24 23 22 21 20   5 4 3 2 1

TEXT AND ILLUSTRATIONS © 2020 JORRIEN PETERSON
THIS BOOK WAS TYPESET IN ARGONE.
THE ILLUSTRATIONS WERE CREATED DIGITALLY.

PUBLISHED BY
GIBBS SMITH
P.O. BOX 667
LAYTON, UTAH 84041

1.800.835.4993 ORDERS
WWW.GIBBS-SMITH.COM

DESIGNED BY KATIE JENNINGS
MANUFACTURED IN SHENZHEN, CHINA IN JANUARY 2020 BY CRASH PAPER.

GIBBS SMITH BOOKS ARE PRINTED ON EITHER RECYCLED, 100% POST-CONSUMER WASTE, FSC-CERTIFIED PAPERS OR ON PAPER PRODUCED FROM SUSTAINABLE PEFC-CERTIFIED FOREST/CONTROLLED WOOD SOURCE. LEARN MORE AT WWW.PEFC.ORG.

LIBRARY OF CONGRESS CATALOGING-IN-PUBLICATION DATA

NAMES: PETERSON, JORRIEN, AUTHOR, ILLUSTRATOR.
TITLE: SEEK & FIND BIOMES : TUNDRA, ALPINE, FOREST, RAINFOREST, SAVANNA, GRASSLAND, DESERT, FRESHWATER, MARINE / JORRIEN PETERSON.
OTHER TITLES: SEEK AND FIND BIOMES : TUNDRA ALPINE FOREST RAINFOREST SAVANNA GRASSLAND DESERT FRESHWATER MARINE
DESCRIPTION: FIRST EDITION. | LAYTON, UTAH : GIBBS SMITH, [2020]. |
   AUDIENCE: AGES 4-10 | SUMMARY: "LEARN ABOUT THE PLANTS AND ANIMALS IN NINE UNIQUE BIOMES WITH FUN FACTS, ENGAGING QUESTIONS, AND INTRICATE ILLUSTRATIONS. A HELPFUL GLOSSARY PROVIDES DETAILS FOR FURTHER DISCOVERY"-- PROVIDED BY PUBLISHER.
IDENTIFIERS: LCCN 2019032158 | ISBN 9781423654032 (HARDCOVER) | ISBN 9781423654049 (EPUB)
SUBJECTS: LCSH: NATURE--JUVENILE LITERATURE. | BIOTIC COMMUNITIES--JUVENILE LITERATURE. | ECOLOGY--JUVENILE LITERATURE. | BIOLOGY--JUVENILE LITERATURE.
CLASSIFICATION: LCC QH541.14 .P48 2020 | DDC 577.8/2--DC23
LC RECORD AVAILABLE AT HTTPS://LCCN.LOC.GOV/2019032158

CONTENTS

INTRODUCTION

 **TUNDRA**

 **ALPINE**

FOREST

RAINFOREST

SAVANNA

 GRASSLAND

DESERT

FRESHWATER

MARINE

GLOSSARY

INTRODUCTION

Welcome to *Seek & Find Biomes*!
You may be asking yourself, "What is a biome?"

A biome is just a fancy term for a community of plants, animals, and even weather, found in one kind of place.

Not everyone agrees on how many biomes there are. Some scientists classify biomes broadly, and others are more precise. In this book, the Earth is divided into nine types of biomes, with a real-life example for each one.

Weather in each biome can sometimes create problems for plants and animals. When plants and animals have to change in order to solve a problem, it is called *adaptation*.

Plants and animals can adapt to their surroundings in a variety of ways. The unique environment within each biome meets the needs of every plant and animal in it, including you! Even biomes far from our home help to control the ecosystem we live in, produce the oxygen we breathe, and grow the food we eat.

This book is full of stories of adaptation of plants, animals, and weather within specific biomes.

Are you ready to explore your world, near and far, top to bottom?

Each biome featured in this book contains specific illustrations of plants and animals for you to seek and find. Use the key at the bottom of each page to guide your search. For an extra challenge, see if you can find the icons below—there's one of each hidden in every biome illustration. Good luck!

TUNDRA

THE BARREN GROUNDS // CANADA

A **tundra** is a cold, treeless plain. The sun doesn't shine on the **Barren Grounds** in Canada regularly. This lack of daylight makes it a pretty cold place to be!

Sunlight is vital for plants to grow. The **Arctic poppy** continually turns to face the sun to get the light and warmth it needs.

The tundra is so cold that animals need to find ways to stay warm. **Arctic bumblebees** shiver their muscles until they are warm enough to fly! **What do you do to get warm?**

SEEK & FIND the plants and animals shown here, all of which can be found in the Barren Grounds biome in Canada.

- **3 ARCTIC BUMBLEBEES**
- **3 ARCTIC WILLOWS**
- **1 ARCTIC FOX**
- **3 CARIBOU**
- **3 ARCTIC HARES**
- **2 LEMMINGS**
- **3 MUSK OXEN**
- **3 ARCTIC POPPIES**
- **1 POLAR BEAR**

ALPINE

THE KHUMBU REGION // NEPAL

The **alpine** biome is found high in the mountains. With that kind of elevation, the **Khumbu region** doesn't have very much oxygen, which limits life. The high elevation also means dangerous levels of sun exposure.

Not many animals have adjusted to life in this extreme environment. **Yaks** combat thin air with their big, big lungs to bring more oxygen into their bodies.

Plants in this alpine biome have learned to handle the harsh sun. **Lichen** can turn red, which helps absorb the sun's rays. **How do you avoid too much sun when it's hot out?**

SEEK & FIND the plants and animals shown here, all of which can be found in the Khumbu region biome in Nepal.

2 BAR-HEADED GEESE

3 HIMALAYAN TAHRS

3 HIMALAYAN BLUE POPPIES

1 HIMALAYAN WOLF

2 HIMALAYAN BLUE SHEEP

2 LICHEN

1 SNOW LEOPARD

2 HIMALAYAN MONALS

3 YAKS

FOREST

DALARNA // SWEDEN

A **forest** is an area of land that is made up of trees. **Dalarna** experiences four distinct seasons each year. These changes in weather require creative ways to survive.

Plants in Dalarna thrive in the warmth and survive in the cold. Unlike trees that lose their leaves, **pines** have needles with a waxy coating that protects them during the cold, cold winter.

Long winters reduce food sources. **Wolverines** store their food in the snow to keep it fresh, kind of like using a refrigerator! **Which favorite food would you want to keep fresh in the winter?**

SEEK & FIND the plants and animals shown here, all of which can be found in the Dalarna biome in Sweden.

- 1 BEAVER
- 2 BIRCH TREES
- 2 BLUEBERRIES
- 2 BROWN BEARS
- 2 LINGONBERRIES
- 2 LYNX
- 3 MOOSE
- 2 PINE TREES
- 2 WOLVERINES

RAINFOREST

DAINTREE // AUSTRALIA

A **rainforest** is a dense area of trees that receives a lot of rain. **Daintree Rainforest** supports a great deal of life, which brings plenty of competition for food and shelter. Around 79 inches of rain fall on **Daintree** each year. That's a lot of water!

With so much competition, animals learn to act differently than their rivals. **Tree kangaroos** hop through trees to avoid predators on the ground.

Too much water can be harmful to plants. The **Bolwarra tree** has waxy leaves that repel excess rain to avoid rotting. **How do you stay dry when it rains?**

SEEK & FIND the plants and animals shown here, all of which can be found in the Daintree Rainforest biome in Australia.

- **2 BOLWARRA TREES**
- **1 CASSOWARY**
- **2 CROCODILES**
- **1 FAN PALM TREE**
- **3 IDIOT FRUIT TREES**
- **3 PLATYPUSES**
- **1 TREE KANGAROO**
- **2 ULYSSES BUTTERFLIES**
- **1 WALLABY**

SAVANNA

THE SERENGETI // TANZANIA

A **savanna** is a warm grassy area, with scattered trees. The **Serengeti** only has two seasons: wet and dry! The wet season helps plants to grow; the dry season causes animals to travel in search of food.

Plants in the savanna survive by adapting to the two extreme seasons. The **baobab tree** has thick, spongy bark that can absorb water really fast during the wet season and store it during the dry season.

Animals of the Serengeti are always on the move. **Wildebeests** travel 1,800 miles each year in search of food. To protect themselves from predators as they go, they migrate in big groups called herds. **Who would you choose to travel 1,800 miles with?**

SEEK & FIND the plants and animals shown here, all of which can be found in the Serengeti biome in Tanzania.

- **3 ACACIA TREES**
- **3 BAOBAB TREES**
- **1 BLACK MAMBA**
- **2 CHEETAHS**
- **2 ELEPHANTS**
- **2 GIRAFFES**
- **2 LIONS**
- **3 WILDEBEESTS**
- **2 ZEBRAS**

GRASSLAND

THE EURASIAN STEPPE // FROM HUNGARY TO CHINA

A **grassland** is a large, flat area of grass. The **Eurasian Steppe** is exposed to rain, drought, snow, and fire. These harsh conditions make it dangerous for animals to stay in one place for long.

Grass here is often flooded, dried, frozen, and burned. Sturdy root systems allow grass to survive these challenges each year.

Animals here must travel a very long way to find new food sources. **Saiga antelope** can smell their food (fresh plants) from more than 100 miles away! **What do you wish you could smell from 100 miles away?**

SEEK & FIND the plants and animals shown here, all of which can be found in the Eurasian Steppe biome, from Hungary to China.

3 BOBAC MARMOTS

1 CORSAC FOX

3 GRASSES

2 MONGOLIAN GERBILS

2 ONAGERS

1 PRZEWALSKI'S HORSE

2 SAIGA ANTELOPE

2 SAKER FALCONS

2 TUMBLEWEEDS

DESERT

THE SONORAN DESERT // MEXICO & UNITED STATES

A **desert** receives very little rain. **The Sonoran Desert** collects less than 15 inches of rain each year. That's not very much! The temperature is hot, hot, hot during the day but gets very cold at night.

Desert plants have unique ways of finding (and saving) water in order to survive. The roots of a 35-foot tall **velvet mesquite tree** stretch three times its size into the ground to search for water.

The animals who call the desert home also have to cleverly adapt to their surroundings. In such hot conditions, the **roadrunner** chooses to run instead of fly to use less energy. **What would you do to save energy?**

SEEK & FIND the plants and animals shown here, all of which can be found in the Sonoran Desert biome in Mexico and the US.

- **1 BIGHORN SHEEP**
- **3 GIANT SAGUAROS**
- **2 GOPHER TORTOISES**
- **1 JAGUAR**
- **3 KANGAROO RATS**
- **2 PALO VERDES**
- **2 ROADRUNNERS**
- **1 SPADEFOOT TOAD**
- **2 VELVET MESQUITE TREES**

FRESHWATER

THE AMAZON RIVER // PERU, ECUADOR, COLOMBIA, BOLIVIA, VENEZUELA & BRAZIL

The **freshwater** biome occurs in bodies of water with very little salt. The **Amazon River** has a very strong current. That means the water moves fast, fast, fast! This constant movement stirs up mud, making the water turn brown.

The fast river current makes it hard for plants to stay rooted. The **Amazon water lily** grows long stems that anchor to the river bottom.

It can be difficult to see through the dark, murky water. The **electric eel** can't see very well to begin with, so it uses an electric field to sense its surroundings. **How would you find your way in the dark?**

SEEK & FIND the plants and animals shown here, all of which can be found in the Amazon River biome in South America.

2 AMAZON RIVER DOLPHINS

1 AMAZON WATER LILY

1 ANACONDA

2 ARAPAIMAS

1 BULL SHARK

2 CAIMANS

1 ELECTRIC EEL

3 MANATEES

3 PIRANHAS

MARINE

THE MESOAMERICAN REEF // MEXICO, BELIZE, GUATEMALA & HONDURAS

The **marine** biome exists in the ocean. Being in the ocean means that the **Mesoamerican Reef** has very salty water. It sits in shallow water, which brings lots of sunlight and crashing waves to the plants and animals below.

Too much salt can make marine animals sick. **Hawksbill sea turtles** have salt glands that pass extra salt through their eyes, like tears.

Sunlight and waves are good, but too much can be harmful for ocean plants. **Seaweed** is so tough it can be dried by the sun and ripped by the waves and still survive. **What would you need to survive underwater?**

SEEK AND FIND the plants and animals shown here, all of which can be found in the Mesoamerican Barrier Reef biome in North America.

- **2 BRAIN CORAL**
- **3 RAINBOW PARROTFISH**
- **2 BUTTERFLYFISH**
- **1 TRUMPETFISH**
- **3 HAWKSBILL SEA TURTLES**
- **2 WHALE SHARKS**
- **1 LEMON SHARK**
- **2 SEAWEEDS**
- **3 MANGROVES**

GLOSSARY

Acacia trees grow in the savanna, surviving in 122° F (50° C) temperatures during the day. They grow thorns up to four inches long to prevent predators from eating them.

Alpine biomes are found at an altitude of 10,000 feet (3,000 m) or higher and lie just below the snow lines of mountains. The Latin word for "Alpine" is "Alps," which means "high mountain." Animals and plants adapt to the extreme cold and intense ultraviolet wavelengths from the sun.

The **Amazon River** in South America is one of the longest rivers in the world. There are over 2,500 known species of fish that live in the river, and scientists keep discovering more.

Amazon river dolphins are the largest species of dolphin—adult males reach up to 408 pounds (185 kg). These dolphins are born gray and turn pink as they get older. When they are excited or surprised, they will blush even more pink, just like humans!

Amazon water lilies grow long stems that anchor the flowers to the muddy river bottoms. These lilies have large, circular leaves that can grow up to 10 feet (3 m) wide.

Anacondas are snakes that can swim in the Amazon River. Their eyes and nostrils are on the tops of their heads, allowing them to see above the water while the rest of their body hides. The largest anaconda recorded was 30 feet (9 m) long.

Arapaimas are air-breathing fish found in the Amazon River. They are also one of the world's largest freshwater fish, growing to be as heavy as 440 pounds (200 kg).

Arctic bumblebees are fuzzy, social bees found in the tundra, and one of only two types of bumblebees that live above the Arctic Circle. By shivering their flight muscles, these hardy bumblebees can raise their internal body temperature to 100.4 °F (38° C) in the cold.

Arctic foxes are found in the Arctic Circle, spanning from Alaska all the way to Russia. They have the warmest skin (called "pelt") of any arctic animal, and their rounded ears, short muzzle, and short legs help them stay warm.

Arctic hares populate northern Greenland, Canada, and the Canadian Arctic Islands. They are colored white to blend in with the snow, and they can run up to 40 miles per hour (64 km/h).

Arctic poppies are tough plants that can survive the coldest Arctic conditions. These flowers continually turn toward the sun, and they grow on rocks that absorb heat from the sun and keep their roots protected.

Arctic willows are tiny shrubs in the tundra that often only grow to be 6 inches (15 cm) tall. Many animals feed on the willows, but they're useful for humans, too. In the past, these willows were used to make medicine that relieved toothaches, helped stop bleeding, and eased stomachaches.

Baobab trees grow in low-lying areas in Africa and Australia. Their bark is shiny to reflect the sun. Some of these trees get very big—there is a very ancient one in Zimbabwe that is more than 70 feet (21 m) tall!

Bar-headed geese are one of the world's highest-flying birds, migrating over the Himalayans each year. They have extra-large hearts to pump oxygen, so they can fly over the high mountains without getting dizzy.

The Barren Grounds are located principally in Nunavut in northern Canada, spreading up into the Northwest Territories. The ground is permanently frozen and the high-speed winds are very cold, but hardy animals and plants still make this land their home. Tourists even visit to go fishing, canoeing, and wilderness camping.

Beavers are found all across North America, Europe, and Asia, and they are the second-largest rodents in the world. Beavers have see-through eyelids that act as goggles to protect their eyes.

Bighorn sheep can weight up to 280 pounds (127 kg). In the Sonoran Desert, they use their horns to smash through barrel cactus to get the water inside.

Birch trees populate forests all around North America, Europe, and Asia. Their flexible branches can bend with the wind and snow to keep them from breaking.

The black mamba is the world's deadliest snake, inhabiting a wide range in sub-Saharan Africa. Its hood flares out when it feels threatened, so it can appear larger. Its venom is so potent that symptoms often appear in only 10 minutes after a bite.

Blueberries are perennial flowering plants with blue and purple berries that typically grow in North America, South America, and Europe. The blue color attracts insects and animals to pollinate and eat, and it also protects against the sun's rays.

Bobac marmots are found on the steppes of Eastern Europe and Central Asia. They live in communities, with one marmot always on watch. When a predator is spotted, the watchman whistles loudly to warn the others.

While the bolwarra tree of Australia often grows between 10 and 16 feet (3 to 5 m) tall, larger specimens may grow up to 50 feet (15 m) tall.

Brain coral, which are found in shallow warm-water coral reefs all over the world, can live for 900 years! Their tentacles catch food at night, then wrap over the coral for protection during the day. Their outside surface is hard, protecting them from fish and hurricanes.

Brown bears are some of the largest bears in the world, weighing up to 800 pounds (360 kg). They enjoy a diverse diet, eating nuts and berries, moths and moose. They might eat up to 40,000 moths in one day!

Bull sharks are found in oceans and rivers all over the world. These sharks have unique kidneys and special glands near their tails to help keep salt in their bodies so they can survive in fresh water.

Butterflyfish are mostly found swimming in the reefs of the Atlantic, Indian, and Pacific Oceans. The name comes from the brightly colored patterns all over their bodies. These brilliant colors fade at night to help butterflyfish blend in with the dark reefs.

Caimans live in the marshes, swamps, rivers, and lakes of Mexico, Central America, and South America. They have very dark skin, which helps keep them hidden when they hunt at night.

Caribou travel in large, migratory herds throughout the tundras. They are born for life on the move: their babies can walk thirty minutes after birth! Their special hooves can act as snowshoes in the snow, paddles in the water, and shovels in the dirt.

Cassowaries are flightless birds, native to the New Guinea, East Nusa Tenggara, the Maluku Islands, and northeastern Australia. Often called "the world's most dangerous bird" because of their tendency to charge, peck, and even headbutt, cassowaries have deep black plumage that helps them blend in with the shadows of the forest.

Cheetahs live primarily in Africa, though some have been found in Iran. They are capable of reaching running speeds up to 70 miles per hour (112 km/h) in only three seconds, making them the fastest land animal.

Corsac foxes are medium-size foxes found in Central Asia. They are nomadic, hunting insects and small rodents at night. They live in abandoned tunnels made by marmots, so they don't have to dig their own deep tunnels.

Crocodiles found in Daintree Rainforest are saltwater crocodiles. Crocodiles are some of the oldest creatures on the entire planet, dating back 240 million years!

The **Daintree Rainforest** spans 460 square miles (740 km²) and is part of the largest continuous area of tropical rainforest on the Australian continent. It houses one of the most complex tropical rainforest ecosystems on Earth.

Dalarna is a historical province in central Sweden. Meaning "the dales," Dalarna is filled with mountainous country, deep and rich forests, glacier-created lakes, and copper mines. Sweden's largest waterfall, the 305-foot (92-m) Njupeskär, is located in Dalarna's Fulufjället National Park.

Desert biomes are barren lands with little precipitation, generally receiving less than 10 inches (2.5 cm) of rain a year. Including polar deserts (also called "cold deserts"), arid and semi-arid regions make up one-third of the world's land surface.

Electric eels are South American fish and the only species in the genus. They're very strong—they can generate a power of 600 volts, which is enough of a shock to knock out a horse!

Elephants roam throughout sub-Saharan Africa, South Asia, and Southeast Asia in many different biomes, including savannas, forests, and deserts. The male elephants in the savanna can weight more than 2,000 pounds (900 kg); they use their large ears to let heat escape so they can stay cool.

The **Eurasian Steppe** is vast, stretching thousands of miles across Europe and Asia, reaching almost 1/5 of the way around Earth. The Steppe experiences cold winters and hot summers.

Fan palm trees flourish throughout the Daintree Rainforest, especially in the Valley of Palms. The palm leaves are split to keep the wind from damaging them.

The Forest biome is the largest land biome, covering about 30 percent of the Earth's land surface. Its ecosystem is filled with trees and underbrush, all of which help balance the Earth's carbon and provide living creatures with oxygen.

The Freshwater biome is defined by its lack of salt. Less than 3 percent of the Earth's water is freshwater, including lakes, ponds, rivers, streams, and wetlands. This water can come from rainfall, melted snow, and melted glaciers.

Giant saguaro can grow to be more than 40 feet (12 m) tall. As these flowering cacti absorb hundreds of gallons of water during the rainy season, their skin expands, like an accordion!

Giraffes are the tallest living land animal. They only need 30 minutes of sleep each day, often for just 5 minutes at a time! They sleep in such shorts bursts to avoid a predator's attack.

Gopher tortoises are native to the southeastern United States. The burrows of these excellent diggers provide shelter for more than 360 other animal species!

Grass is considered "the great survivor"—it can be frozen, burned, or over-grazed and still survive. It is also one of the most versatile plant life forms, and an important food source for many animals.

Grassland biomes experience extreme temperatures, with hot summers over 100 °F (38° C) and freezing winters under -40° F (-40° C). These lands are not wet enough for trees to grow, but early American settlers found grass as high as eleven feet tall.

Hawksbill sea turtles appear in oceans all around the world's equator. Their shells can change color depending on whether they are swimming in warm or cold water.

Himalayan blue poppies are found in only remote areas of the Himalayas. They are delicate flowers that take 2 or 3 years to bloom. Once they produce seeds, they wither quickly and die.

Himalayan blue sheep have blue-gray coats that act as a camouflage in the cold mountains. They're actually not sheep at all, but are described as "goats with sheeplike traits."

Himalayan monals are found throughout the Himalayas and are the national bird of Nepal. Their long, curved beaks can dig in the hard soil of the mountains for food.

Himalayan tahrs stay warm with thick, reddish wool coats and thick undercoats. Their hooves have rubbery cores that give them a good grip on steep mountainsides.

Himalayan wolves are found throughout India, China, Mongolia, and Nepal in small packs of 6 to 8 members. They have adapted to the high altitudes and their hearts can process oxygen more efficiently than other wolves.

Idiot fruit trees, known as the "green dinosaur," are one of the most ancient species of trees on the planet. Scientists have matched fossils from 120 million years ago to specimens today with almost no changes—making the idiot fruit tree twice as old as the Tyrannosaurus rex!

Jaguars are native to the Americas. Their incredibly powerful jaws are strong enough to pierce skulls and crack sea turtle shells. They can swim, climb, and navigate many terrains, making them a dangerous hunter.

Kangaroo rats are found in the desert. Their long tails and big hind feet enable them to jump distances of 9 feet (2.75 m)! They can survive without drinking water, getting enough moisture out of the seeds they eat.

The Khumbu region is in northeastern Nepal, spanning from 11,000 feet (3,350 m) to the highest place on earth—29,029 feet (8,848 m)! And it's still growing! The mountain inches up 4 millimeters every year because of the rocks shifting beneath it.

Lemmings are small rodents normally found in the Arctic. They are brown in the summer and white in the winter, and they have long front claws for digging tunnels in the ground and snow.

Lemon sharks are found on the shores of North America, South America, and Africa. They are dark gray and blue on top and white on the bottom, allowing them to blend in with the scenery from above *and* below.

Lichen is made up of fungi and algae that grow together in a symbiotic relationship. Its tissues can survive frost and long periods without water, which may be why it's among the oldest living things on the planet.

Lingonberry bushes populate much of the Northern Hemisphere, sprawling from Europe and Asia to North America. The fungi that grow on its roots helps this evergreen shrub break down nutrients quickly.

Lions live in the savannas in sub-Saharan Africa. They have impressive night vision—6 times more sensitive to light than humans—and they can rotate their ears toward the direction noise is coming from.

Lynx have unique tufts of fur on their ears to help enhance hearing, and their vision is sharp: a lynx can see a mouse from 250 feet (76 m) away.

Manatees inhabit shallow, marshy coastal areas and can weigh up to 1,300 pounds (590 kg). They stick to warm water and spend almost half their day eating sea grass, mangrove leaves, and algae. They can rest underwater, holding their breath, for up to 20 minutes.

Mangroves are shrubs or small trees. They provide habitat for fish and shorebirds, and their roots stick out of the water in order to breathe.

The Marine biome, made up of our oceans, is the largest biome on Earth, covering about 71 percent of the planet. Half of all species on our planet live in the ocean. Scientists think that we have only explored 5 percent of the ocean floor, so much of this biome remains a mystery.

The Mesoamerican Reef is the largest barrier reef in the Western Hemisphere. This reef is home to 65 species of coral, 350 species of mollusk, and more than 500 species of fish!

Mongolian gerbils are clever to escape predators. They give off less odor than other rodents to avoid detection, and if caught by their tail, they can shed it quickly to escape.

Moose are found in North America, Europe, and Asia. These huge herbivores, sometimes weighing up to 1,500 pounds (680 kg), will travel downwind before stopping to rest so they can smell if a predator is tracking them.

Musk oxen thrive in the coldest regions, their long shaggy coat and undercoat keeping them warm. When threatened by predators, the herd gathers in a circle to protect the young.

Onagers live in deserts and other dry regions. While onagers get water from the plants they eat, they can also dig holes in dry riverbeds to find water, which helps many other animals find water, too.

Palo Verde are known as nurse trees: they shelter smaller and slow-growing trees or plants by providing shade, shelter, and protection. In the Sonoran Desert, Palo Verde act as nurse trees for young saguaro cacti.

Pine trees are so common in the Northern Hemisphere that almost every region has some native species of pine. These trees typically reach ages from 100 to 1,000 years old, and sometimes live even longer. They are made to last: their pine cones protect seeds from harsh cold and their dark color helps them absorb more sun.

Piranhas are freshwater fish in South America. These fish have razor sharp teeth. Despite their reputation, they don't just eat meat—piranhas eat animals, plants, seeds, and fruit, which makes them omnivores!

Platypuses are unique to Australia, and one of the most distinct animals on the Earth. Not only do they *not* have a stomach, but their bills can sense the electric fields of other creatures, enabling them to hunt with their eyes, ears, and nose closed!

Polar bears have an incredibly strong sense of smell that allows them to smell food from 20 miles (32 km) away! They can even smell seals through the ice. Their large paws are adapted for swimming, and they can swim for days at a time.

Przewalski's horses roam the steppes of central Asia, and are the last truly wild horse still in existence. In the harsh winters, they grow thick, warm coats, and will turn their backs to high winds and tuck their tails between their legs to protect themselves from the cold.

Rainbow parrotfish save energy by not swimming against the waves; instead they use the motion of the waves to help them move along to find food.

The Rainforest biome is the Earth's oldest living ecosystem. Home to half of the terrestrial world's plant and animal species, the rainforest is so vast that there may still be millions of plants, insects, and microorganisms still undiscovered. The rainforest is responsible for almost a third of the world's oxygen turnover.

Roadrunners are found in the deserts of southwestern United States and Mexico. These speedy birds are so fast that they are one of the few animals that can hunt rattlesnakes.

Saiga antelope are found in Russia and Kazakhstan today, roaming the foothills and steppes. Their famous hanging nose acts as a filter: it prevents dust particles from entering their lungs and regulates the temperature of the air they breathe.

Saker falcons are large birds of prey that hunt in southeast Europe and Asia, as well as Africa during the winter. Despite being only 18 inches (45 cm) tall, these falcons are fierce predators: they can dive for their prey at 200 miles per hour (322 km/h).

Savannas are rolling grasslands with sparse shrubs and isolated trees. The plants of the savannas become specialized to grow in long periods of drought, and the animals are adapted to journey on long migrations.

Seaweed is not actually a plant at all—seaweed is a type of algae, with no roots, stems, or leaves. Each seaweed cell takes what it needs from the seawater around it. About 70 percent of the world's oxygen comes from seaweed and algae.

The **Serengeti** ecosystem is located in northern Tanzania, spanning about 12,000 square miles (19,000 km^2). It is one of the Seven Natural Wonders of Africa because of its mammal migration, which is the second largest in the world. It is thriving with diversity, with 70 large mammal species, 500 bird species, and many different habitats.

Snow leopards are found in northern and central Asia. Often called the "ghosts of the mountain" because they are so rare, they have thick, massive tails that help them maintain balance on rocky ridges.

The **Sonoran Desert**, which spans southwestern United States and northwestern Mexico, is the hottest desert in North America—the temperatures in the summer often reach 118° F (48° C). Despite the heat, the desert is still home to plenty of life, with 100 species of reptiles, 20 species of amphibians, 60 species of mammals, and more than 350 types of birds.

Spadefoot toads are native to North America. They use their spade-like feet to dig burrows and will stay underground for weeks at a time.

Tree kangaroos live in the rainforests of Papua New Guinea, Indonesia, and Australia. They move from treetop to treetop easily thanks to their long tails, and they can leap distances of 30 feet (9 m)—in fact, they're so good at jumping that they can fall 60 feet (18 m) without being hurt!

Trumpetfish primarily live in reefs. These clever fish float vertically among coral to blend in and surprise prey. Their mouths become wide and round so they can vacuum up their food.

Tumbleweeds are seen most commonly in steppes and dry regions, where the wind and flat ground allow them to roll easily. These plants break off of their base when they're mature and allow themselves to be blown around. The act of rolling spreads the seeds of the plant.

Tundra biomes are found in the far Northern Hemisphere, up around the Arctic Circle. Around 20 percent of the Earth is tundra, and these regions are very barren, with freezing climates, low biological diversity, short growth seasons, and simple vegetation.

Ulysses butterflies are known for the iridescent blue on their wings. Because their coloring makes them easy to spot, they fly in fast, unpredictable flight patterns to avoid being caught by predators.

Velvet mesquite trees are native to the Sonoran, Mojave, and Chihuahuan Deserts. To survive the dry desert, the roots of the tree dig deep into the earth, far deeper than the height of the tree, to find water.

Wallabies are marsupials native to Australia and New Guinea. Though they're smaller than kangaroos, they still deliver powerful kicks to fend off predators, and their tails are used for balance and support.

Whale sharks are not whales at all, despite the name. Found in the world's tropical oceans, they are docile, slow-moving sharks that are filter feeders: water goes in and out through gill slits; food makes it through the filter and unwanted items do not.

Wildebeests are massive members of the antelope family, sometimes weighing up to 600 pounds (272 kg). Found across Africa, particularly in the Serengeti, they herd together with zebra. The zebras have sharper senses, but the wildebeests are stronger, so they work together as a team to survive.

Wolverines are found throughout the forest, alpine, and tundra biomes of the Northern Hemisphere. Their paws are incredibly versatile—not only are they good climbers and good swimmers, but their paws expand to twice the normal size when they step, acting as a snowshoe.

Yaks are heavy, bulky animals native to the Himalayas, with sturdy legs, huge hooves, and shaggy hair. Their thick horns can break through frozen snow to get to the plants underneath, as well as help them defend themselves.

Zebras roam various habitats, such as grasslands, savannas, woodlands, mountains, and coastal hills. Their stripes make them difficult to see while in a herd and blur their escape while they run from predators.

ANSWER KEY

TUNDRA

ALPINE

FOREST

RAINFOREST

SAVANNA

GRASSLAND

DESERT

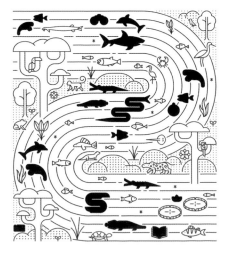

FRESHWATER

MARINE

Jorrien Peterson is one half of the husband and wife design duo Fell. Jorrien's work has been featured in the Communication Arts Illustration Annual, the Association of Illustrators World Illustration Awards, and his mother's refrigerator. He lives in the mountains of Utah with his wife and is adapting to having two children. This is his first book.